KEEPSAKES

CHILDREN

D0170841

CLB 4393
Published 1995 by CLB Publishing
Exclusively for Selectabook Ltd, Devizes
© 1995 CLB Publishing, Godalming, Surrey
ISBN 1-85833-298-2

Printed in Hong Kong by Imago

KEEPSAKES

CHILDREN

Compiled by
Virginia Farr

SELECT
EDITIONS

Down to the Beach

As THE MORNING lengthened whole parties appeared over the sand-hills and came down on the beach to bathe. It was understood that at eleven o'clock the women and children of the summer colony had the sea to themselves. First the women undressed, pulled on their bathing dresses and covered their heads in hideous caps like sponge-bags; then the children were unbuttoned. The little Trout boys whipped their shirts over their heads, and away the five sped . . . .

The firm compact little girls were not half so brave as the tender, delicate-looking little boys. Pips and Rags, shivering, crouching down, slapping the water, never hesitated. But Isabel, who could swim twelve strokes, and Kezia, who could nearly swim eight, only followed on the strict understanding they were not to be splashed. As for Lottie, she didn't follow at all. She liked to be left to go in her own way, please. And that way was to sit down at the edge of the water, her legs straight, her knees pressed together, and to make vague motions with her arms as if she expected to be wafted out to sea. But when a bigger wave than usual, an old whiskery one, came lolloping along in her direction, she scrambled to her feet with a face of horror and flew up the beach again.

KATHERINE MANSFIELD

Pied Piper's Progress

Once more he stepped into the street,
    And to his lips again
Laid his long pipe of smooth straight cane,
    And ere he blew three notes (such sweet
Soft notes as yet musician's cunning
    Never gave the enraptured air)
There was a rustling, that seemed like a bustling
    Of merry crowds jostling at pitching and hustling,
Small feet were pattering, wooden shoes clattering,
    Little hands clapping and little tongues chattering,
And, like fowls in a farmyard when barley is scattering,
    Out came the children running.
All the little boys and girls,
    With rosy cheeks and flaxen curls,
And sparkling eyes and teeth like pearls,
    Tripping and skipping, ran merrily after
The wonderful music with shouting and laughter.

ROBERT BROWNING

Talking of Children

HE REVEREND Doctor was unfortunately deaf, but Mrs Hughes made amends for all her good-natured husband's failings by her tact and gracious volubility.... Lady Scott and she conversed about their families, and Sir Walter seemed to take the opportunity of expressing his mind about his son Charles, who he said was wasting his precious time from morning to night every day, either fishing or shooting.... Then turning to me, he said, 'I observe that Sir Joshua Reynolds was very fond of children, and the children reciprocated his feelings. He used to play with them, and he delighted to amuse them – would roll himself on the carpet, and become himself a boy, with all the fun and joy and laughter of childhood.... For myself, I have often tried to ingratiate myself with the innocent, dear little things. I admire their beauty, and enjoy their pretty prattle, but some-how or other I never seem to make a favourable impression. I do not succeed with them, they do not approach me with the familiarity or favour that they show to other men. I am sure I have often tried to take pains enough to gain their good opinion, and I would do anything to obtain their confidence and love.'

WILLIAM BEWICK

Waiting for Sleep

AT HALF PAST NINE that night, Tom and Sid were sent to bed . . . . and Sid was soon asleep. Tom lay awake and waited in restless impatience. When it seemed to him that it must be nearly daylight, he heard the clock strike ten! This was despair. He would have tossed and fidgeted, as his nerves demanded, but he was afraid he might wake Sid. So he lay still and stared up into the dark. Everything was dismally still. By-and-by, out of the stillness little scarcely perceptible noises began to emphasize themselves. The ticking of the clock began to bring itself into notice. Old beams began to crack mysteriously. The stairs creaked faintly. Evidently spirits were abroad. A measured, muffled snore issued from Aunt Polly's chamber. And now the tiresome chirping of a cricket that no human ingenuity could locate began. Next the ghastly ticking of a death-watch in the wall at the bed's head made Tom shudder – it meant that somebody's days were numbered. Then the howl of a far-off dog rose on the night air and was answered by a fainter howl from a remoter distance. Tom was in an agony. At last he was satisfied that time had ceased and eternity begun; he began to doze in spite of himself; the clock chimed eleven, but he did not hear it.

MARK TWAIN

Innocence

I fear to love thee, Sweet, because
    Love's the ambassador of loss;
White flake of childhood, clinging so
    To my soiled raiment, thy shy snow
At tenderest touch will shrink and go.
    Love me not, delightful child.
My heart, by many snares beguiled,
    Has grown timorous and wild.

Know you what it is to be a child? It is to be something very different from the man of today.

It is to have a spirit yet streaming from the waters of baptism, it is to believe in love, to believe in loveliness, to believe in belief. It is to be so little that the elves can reach to whisper in your ear. It is to turn pumpkins into coaches, and mice into horses, lowness into loftiness and nothing into everything – for each child has his fairy godmother in his own soul. It is to live in a nutshell and count yourself king of the infinite space.

FRANCIS THOMPSON

Naughty Boy

There was a naughty boy,
　And a naughty boy was he,
He ran away to Scotland
　The people for to see –
　　There he found
　　That the ground
　　Was as hard,
　　That a yard
　　Was as long,
　　That a song
　　Was as merry,
　　That a cherry
　　Was as red–
　　That lead
　　Was as weighty
　　That fourscore
　　Was as eighty,
　　That a door
　　Was as wooden
　　As in England–
So he stood in his shoes
　And he wondered.

JOHN KEATS

THE WORLD

Letter to the Editor

Dear Editor
I am 8 years old. Some of my little friends say there is no Santa Claus. Papa
says 'If you see it in the Sun it's so.' Please tell me the truth. Is there a Santa
Claus?

VIRGINIA O'HANLON, 115 WEST 95TH STREET, NEW YORK

Virginia, your little friends are wrong. They have been
affected by the scepticism of a sceptical age.... Yes,
Virginia, there is a Santa Claus. He exists as certainly as love
and generosity and devotion exist, and you know that they
abound and give to your life its highest beauty and joy. Alas!
how dreary would be the world if there were no Santa Claus!
It would be as dreary as if there were no Virginias. There
would be no childlike faith then, no poetry, no romance to
make tolerable this existence. We should have no enjoyment,
except in sense and sight. The eternal light with which
childhood fills the world would be extinguished. Not believe
in Santa Claus! You might as well not believe in fairies!....
No Santa Claus! Thank God! he lives, and lives forever....
ten times ten thousand years from now, he will continue to
make glad the heart of childhood.

NEW YORK SUN, 21 SEPTEMBER 1897

To Her Infant

Now in thy dazzling half-oped eye,
    Thy curlèd nose and lip awry,
Thy up-hoist arms and noddling head,
    And little chin with crystal spread,
Poor helpless thing! what do I see,
    That I should sing of thee?

Thy rosy cheek so soft and warm;
    Thy pinky hand and dimpled arm;
Thy silken locks that scantly peep,
    With gold-tipped ends, where circles deep
Around thy neck in harmless grace
    So soft and sleekly hold their place,
Might harder hearts with kindness fill,
    And gain our right good will.

Perhaps when time shall add a few
    Short years to thee, thou'lt love me too.
Then wilt thou through life's weary way
    Become my sure and cheering stay:
Wilt care for me, and be my hold,
    When I am weak and old.

JOANNA BAILLIE

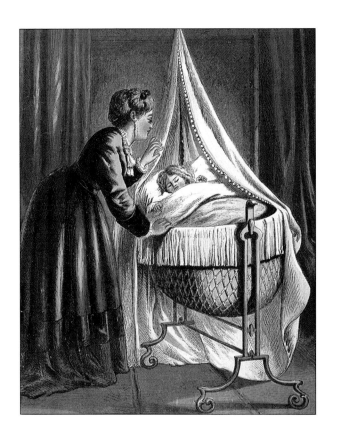

A Child's Wonder

THERE WAS ONCE a child, and he strolled about a good deal, and thought of a number of things. He had a sister, who was a child too, and his constant companion. These two used to wonder all day long. They wondered at the beauty of the flowers; they wondered at the height and blueness of the sky; they wondered at the depth of the bright water; they wondered at the goodness and the power of God who made the lovely world. They used to say to one another, sometimes, Supposing all the children upon earth were to die, would the flowers, and the water, and the sky be sorry? They believed they would be sorry. For, said they, the buds are the children of the flowers, and the little playful streams that gambol down the hillsides are the children of the water; and the smallest bright specks playing at hide and seek in the sky all night must surely be the children of the stars; and they would all be grieved to see their playmates, the children of men, no more.

CHARLES DICKENS

Morning Ritual

Y VACANT attention soon found livelier attraction in the spectacle of a little hungry robin .... The remains of my breakfast of bread and milk stood on the table, and having crumbled a morsel of roll, I was tugging at the sash to put out the crumbs on the window-sill, when Bessie came running upstairs into the nursery.

'Miss Jane, take off your pinafore: what are you doing there? Have you washed your hands and face this morning?' ... Closing the window, I replied –

'No Bessie; I have only just finished dusting.'

'Troublesome, careless child! – and what are you doing now? You look quite red, as if you had been about some mischief: what were you opening the window for?'

I was spared the trouble of answering, for Bessie seemed to be in too great a hurry to listen to explanations; she hauled me to the washstand, inflicted a merciless, but happily brief, scrub on my face and hands with soap, water, and a coarse towel; disciplined my head with a bristly brush, denuded me of my pinafore, and then, hurrying me to the top of the stairs, bid me go down directly, as I was wanted in the breakfast-room.

CHARLOTTE BRONTE

Mrs Pardiggle's Boys

HESE, YOUNG LADIES,' said Mrs Pardiggle, with great volubility, after the first salutations, 'are my five boys.... Egbert, my eldest (twelve), is the boy who sent out his pocket-money, to the amount of five-and-threepence, to the Tockahoopo Indians. Oswald, my second (ten-and-a-half), is the child who contributed two-and-ninepence to the Great National Smithers Testimonial. Francis, my third (nine), one-and-sixpence-halfpenny; Felix, my fourth (seven), eightpence to the Superannuated Widows; Alfred, my youngest (five), has voluntarily enrolled himself in the Infant Bonds of Joy.' ...

We had never seen such dissatisfied children. It was not merely that they were weazened and shrivelled – though they were certainly that too – but they looked absolutely ferocious with discontent. At the mention of the Tockahoopo Indians, I could really have supposed Egbert to be one of the most baleful members of that tribe, he gave me such a savage frown. The face of each child, as the amount of his contribution was mentioned, darkened in a peculiarly vindictive manner, but his was by far the worst. I must except, however, the little recruit into the Infant Bonds of Joy, who was stolidly and evenly miserable.

CHARLES DICKENS

Off to Bed

Golden slumbers kiss your eyes,
　　Smiles awake you when you rise.
Sleep, pretty wantons, do not cry,
　　And I will sing a lullaby.
Rock them, rock them, lullaby.

Care is heavy, therefore sleep you.
　　You are care, and care must keep you.
Sleep, pretty wantons, do not cry,
　　And I will sing a lullaby.
Rock them, rock them, lullaby.

THOMAS DEKKER

In jumping and tumbling
　　We spend the whole day,
Till night by arriving
　　Has finished our play.

What then? One and all,
　　There's no more to be said,
As we tumbled all day
　　So we tumble to bed.

ANONYMOUS, 18TH CENTURY

BE GOOD, AND YOU WILL BE HAPPY.

"HUSH-A-BYE BABY."

Good and Bad Children

Children, you are very little,
    And your bones are very brittle;
If you would grow great and stately,
    You must try to walk sedately.

You must still be bright and quiet,
    And content with simple diet;
And remain, through all bewild'ring,
    Innocent and honest children.

Happy hearts and happy faces,
    Happy play in grassy places –
That was how, in ancient ages,
    Children grew to kings and sages.

But the unkind and the unruly,
    And the sort who eat unduly,
They must never hope for glory –
    Theirs is quite a different story!

Cruel children, crying babies,
    All grow up as geese and gabies,
Hated, as their age increases,
    By their nephews and their nieces.

ROBERT LOUIS STEVENSON

The Christ-Child

The Christ-child lay on Mary's lap,
  His hair was like a light.
(O weary, weary were the world,
  But here is all right.)

The Christ-child lay on Mary's breast,
  His hair was like a star.
(O stern and cunning are the kings,
  But here the true hearts are.)

The Christ-child lay on Mary's heart,
  His hair was like a fire.
(O weary, weary is the world,
  But here the world's desire.)

The Christ-child stood at Mary's knee,
  His hair was like a crown,
And all the flowers looked up at Him,
  And all the stars looked down.

G. K. CHESTERTON

Spoiling

MAY 26, SUNDAY. We went to Sutton after dinner to have meat-tea with Mr and Mrs James. I had no appetite, having dined well at two, and the entire evening was spoiled by little Percy – their only son – who seems to me to be an utterly spoiled child. Two or three times he came up to me and deliberately kicked my shins.... I gently remonstrated with him, and Mrs James said: 'Please don't scold him; I do not believe in being too severe with young children. You spoil their character.' Little Percy set up a deafening yell here, and when Carrie tried to pacify him, he slapped her face. I was so annoyed, I said: 'That is not my idea of bringing up children, Mrs James.'. A very nice gentleman, Mr Birks Spooner, took the child by the wrist and said: 'Come here, dear, and listen to this.' He detached his chronometer from the chain and made his watch strike six. To our horror, the child snatched it from his hand and bounced it down upon the ground like one would a ball. Carrie said the child was bad-tempered, but it made up for that defect by its looks, for it was – in her mind – an unquestionably beautiful child. I may be wrong, but I do not think I have seen a much uglier child myself.

GEORGE AND WEEDON GROSSMITH

Memories of Kate

She was not as pretty as women I know,
And yet all your best made of sunshine
   and snow
Drop to shade, melt to nought in the
   long-trodden ways,
While she's still remembered on warm
   and cold days – My Kate.

Her air had a meaning, her movements a grace,
You turned from the fairest to gaze
   on her face.
And when you had once seen her forehead
   and mouth,
You saw as distinctly her soul
   and her truth – My Kate.

Such a blue inner light from her eyelids outbroke,
You looked at her silence and fancied
   she spoke.
When she did, so peculiar yet soft
   was the tone,
Though the loudest spoke also,
   you heard her alone – My Kate.

ELIZABETH BARRETT BROWNING

The Four Sisters

ARGARET, THE ELDEST of the four, was sixteen, and very pretty, being plump and fair, with large eyes, plenty of soft brown hair, a sweet mouth, and white hands, of which she was rather vain. Fifteen-year-old Jo was very tall, thin, and brown, and reminded one of a colt; for she never seemed to know what to do with her long limbs, which were very much in her way. She had a decided mouth, a comical nose, and sharp grey eyes, which appeared to see everything . . . . Her long, thick hair was her one beauty; but it was usually bundled into a net, to be out of the way. Round shoulders had Jo, big hands and feet . . . . Elizabeth – or Beth, as everyone called her – was a rosy, smooth-haired, bright-eyed girl of thirteen, with a shy manner, a timid voice, and a peaceful expression, which was seldom disturbed. Her father called her 'Little Tranquillity', and the name suited her excellently; for she seemed to live in a happy world of her own, only venturing out to meet the few whom she trusted and loved. Amy, though the youngest, was a most important person, in her own opinion at least. A regular snow-maiden, with blue eyes, and yellow hair curling on her shoulders; pale and slender . . . .

LOUISA M. ALCOTT

Come to Me, Children

Come to me, O ye children!
   For I hear you at your play,
And the questions that perplexed me
   Have vanished quite away.

Ye open the eastern windows,
   That look towards the sun,
Where thoughts are singing swallows
   And the brooks of morning run.

What the leaves are to the forest,
   With light and air for food,
Ere their sweet and tender juices
   Have been hardened into wood,

That to the world are children;
   Through them it feels the glow
Of a brighter and sunnier climate
   Than reaches the trunks below.

Come to me, O ye children!
   And whisper in my ear
What the birds and the winds are singing
   In your sunny atmosphere.

HENRY WADSWORTH LONGFELLOW

A Water Baby

OM WAS AMPHIBIOUS; and what is better still, he was clean. For the first time in his life, he felt how comfortable it was to have nothing on him but himself. But he only enjoyed it: he did not know it, or think about it; just as you enjoy life and health, and yet never think about being alive and healthy . . . .

He did not remember having ever been dirty. Indeed, he did not remember any of his old troubles, being tired, or hungry, or beaten, or sent up dark chimneys. Since that sweet sleep, he had forgotten all about his master, and Harthover Place, and the little white girl, and in a word, all that had happened to him when he lived before; and what was best of all, he had forgotten all the bad words which he had learned from Grimes, and the rude boys with whom he used to play . . . .

Tom was very happy in the water. He had been sadly overworked in the land-world; and so now, to make up for that, he had nothing but holidays in the water-world for a long, long time to come. He had nothing to do now but enjoy himself and look at all the pretty things which are to be seen in the cool clear water-world, where the sun is never too hot, and the frost is never too cold.

CHARLES KINGSLEY

Evening Prayer

O merciful God, hear this our request,
   And grant unto us this night quiet rest.
Into thy tuition O Lord do us take,
   Our bodies sleeping, our minds yet may wake.
Forgive the offences this day we have wrought
   Against thee and our neighbour in word, deed and
      thought.
And grant us thy grace henceforth to fly sin
   And that a new life we may now begin.
Deliver and defend us this night from all evil
   And from the danger of our enemy, the Devil,
Which goeth about seeking his prey
   And by his craft whom we may betray.
Assist us, O Lord, with thy holy sprite,
   That valiantly against him we may ever fight,
And winning the victory may lift up our voice
   And in thy strength faithfully rejoice,
Saying 'To the Lord be all honour and praise
   For his defence both now and always!'

FRANCIS SEAGER

Sources and Acknowledgments

For permission to produce illustrations, the publishers thank the following: Mary Evans Picture Library, Dickens House Museum London, Manchester City Art Galleries, Uffizi Gallery Florence and Sam Elder.